PICASSO
BY

Picasso

Bull's Head, 1943, Musée Picasso, Paris

PICASSO
BY

ARTISTS BY THEMSELVES
EDITED AND WITH AN INTRODUCTION
BY RACHEL BARNES

BRACKEN
BOOKS

Introduction text Copyright ©1990 Rachel Barnes
Series devised by Nicky Bird

This edition published 1992 by The Promotional Reprint
Company Limited exclusively for Bracken Books, an
imprint of Studio Editions Limited, Princess House, 50
Eastcastle Street, London W1N 7AP England.

Reprinted 1994

ISBN 1 85170 981 9

CONTENTS

Introduction 6

Picasso by Picasso 18

Self Portrait 19

Harlequin, Paris Autumn 21

Old Guitarist 23

La Vie, Barcelona 25

Lola, La Soeur de l'Artiste 27

Les Demoiselles d'Avignon 29

Self Portrait 31

Femme à la Mandolin 33

Factory at the Village of Horta de Goro 35

Study for a Construction 37

The Card Player 39

The Violin 41

Portrait of Olga in an Armchair 43

Three Musicians 45

The Lovers 47

Madame Picasso 49

Paolo as a Harlequin 51

Three Dancers 53

Seated Bather 55

Paysage Boisgeloup 57

La Muse 59

La Guernica 60/61

Dora Maar 63

Woman in a Fish Hat 65

La Casserole Emaillée 67

Goat's Skull, Bottle and Candle 69

Bearded Man 71

Jacqueline in a Mantilla 73

The Artist and his Model 75

Self Portrait 77

Chronology 78

Acknowledgements 80

INTRODUCTION

> Everyone wants to understand art. Why not try to understand the songs of a bird? Why does one love the night, flowers, everything around one, without trying to understand them? But in the case of a painting people have to understand. If only they would realize above all that an artist works out of necessity, that he himself is only a trifling bit of the world, and that no more importance should be attached to him than to plenty of other things, things which please us in the world, though we can't explain them.

Picasso made this statement to his friend and biographer Christian Zervos in 1935, by which time he was in his fifties and internationally recognized as one of the greatest of all modern painters. His words reflect his continual response to critics and public, who constantly pestered him for 'the truth' about his paintings.

Picasso remains the most famous and most talked about painter in the recent history of Western art. He lived to be ninety-two and consequently was for many years aware of this extraordinary fame: of being a legend in his own lifetime. But it was essential for his continued development as a painter – and Picasso was inventive and prolific right up until the end of his life – that he should preserve his independence and solitude intact, although from the 1960s onwards the intrusion of the media made such privacy virtually impossible. It was largely as a consequence of this that Picasso became notorious for building up complicated levels of defence,

Child Holding a Dove, 1901, Reproduced by Courtesy of The Trustees, The
National Gallery, London

Girl in a Chemise, 1905, Tate Gallery, London

often deflecting direct questions about himself or his art. One of his biographers, Pierre Daix, once spoke of how Picasso hated to be recorded and recalled how he had told him that he was like a primitive who didn't like to be photographed, to which Picasso replied, 'Exactly!'.

But it was not solely the problems of living as a world-renowned artist in the twentieth century which prompted Picasso's famous reticence – his great friend Henri Matisse had received almost as much attention, and was usually direct and honest when questioned about his intentions as a painter. Rather, it was a part of Picasso's complex and at times introspective personality to develop such an armour. He told Zervos:

It is not what the artist does that counts but what he is. Cézanne would never have interested me a bit if he had lived and thought like Jacques Emile Blanche, even if the apple he painted had been ten times as beautiful. What forces our interest is Cézanne's anxiety – that's Cézanne's lesson; the torments of Van Gogh – that is the actual drama of the man. The rest is a sham.

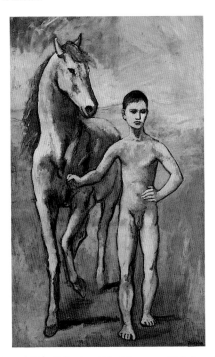

Boy Leading a Horse, 1906, Collection, The Museum of Modern Art, New York, Gift of William S. Paley

Clearly, it was this knowledge that the artist has only himself as his raw material which made it necessary for Picasso to keep himself a little apart. For the reader of his comments on his own art, this poses certain problems. He wrote very little about his paintings, and so most of his reflections have either been recorded in interviews with journalists or quoted by his friends and family. The only statements by Picasso himself are those given to the art critic Marcus de Zayas in 1923, the 1935 statement to his biographer Christian Zervos, and his post-war interview with Jerome Seckler. All three are fascinating documents and provide insight into the artist's work; yet, in these, as in his reported comments, the reader cannot fail to be aware of a number of contradictions. For example, Picasso often said that a painting cannot be thought out beforehand – but not as often as he insisted that nothing in art is an accident. On the subject of success he could also be self contradictory. In the 'fifties he stated that: 'Success is dangerous. One begins to copy oneself, and to copy oneself is more dangerous than to copy others. It leads to sterility.' By 1966, however, he was saying: 'But success is an important thing! It has often been said that an artist should work for himself for the love of his art and scorn success. It's a false idea. An artist needs success.'

Because many of these comments are quoted from a specific conversation, the reader must always be aware of potential confusions which may result from taking Picasso's remarks out of context, bearing in mind that he was quite capable of deliberate perversity, particularly if he found his interviewer too insistent.

Pablo Ruiz Picasso was born in 1881 in Malaga on the Andalusian coast of Spain. His father, José Ruiz Blasco, was an artist who earned his living as a museum curator, an occupation which involved taking his family to Corunna and then, in 1895, to Barcelona.

The young Pablo was the archetypal child prodigy, astounding his parents with his extraordinary precocity. There appears never to have been any doubt that Pablo would grow up to be a painter – one story tells how the boy's father was so amazed at his son's nascent ability that he presented his own palette and brushes to the child, swearing that he himself might as well give up painting altogether.

After briefly attending the Academy in Barcelona, Picasso left to become involved with the intellectual group of Catalan poets and painters who met regularly in a tavern known as Els Quatres Gats. The most vociferous and dominant members were the artist Santiago Rusinol, the critic Miguel Utrillo, the fashionable portraitist Ramon Casas and the painter of outcasts, Isidro Nonell. The avant garde ideas of this set were to have an important influence on Picasso in these early, formative years.

In 1900 Picasso made his first trip to his future home, Paris. He went with his greatest friend of the time, fellow painter Carlos Casegemas who, as the result of an unrequited love affair – or, more specifically, of his own impotence – was tragically to kill himself at the age of only twenty. This sudden death of a close friend was to have a deep and lasting effect on the sensitive and emotional Picasso. The desolation he felt at this early experience of death and despair found expression in what some critics believe to be his finest work – his Blue Period, which lasted until 1904. These mysterious, melancholy paintings, all executed in a monochrome of blue, have distinctly Symbolist, *fin de siècle* overtones. The stark images, expressing themes of poverty, isolation and despair, remain amongst the best known of Picasso's works, most especially 'La Vie' of 1903 (see p25) which is thought to be specifically biographical of his friend Casegemas. Despite their aura of spiritual mystery, these paintings have a stronger emotional impact than many of Picasso's later works, which helps to explain their continued popularity.

The Blue Period was followed by the much briefer Rose Period, before Picasso began on his Saltimbanques which, although different in subject matter, still possess an air of melancholy. It was at this time that Picasso began the first of his important love affairs. Like all Picasso's subsequent passions, Fernande Olivier, who was to be his mistress and model for the next six years, was a great inspiration to his work and the subject of a number of portraits. She later described how he appeared at this time, recalling his image in the 1900 self portrait in Barcelona. He was:

> ... small, black, thick set, restless, disquieting, with eyes dark, profound, piercing, strange, almost staring. Awkward gestures, the hands of a woman, poorly dressed, badly groomed. A thick lock of hair, black and shining, slashed across his intelligent and obstinate forehead. Half bohemian, half workman in his dress, his long hair brushed onto the collar of his worn out jacket.

This period in Paris was a time of hardship and poverty for Picasso, but the friends he was making and the fellow artists he was meeting made it an important one. From these early days the 'bande Picasso' included the sculptors Manolo Gargallo and Gonzalez, and the painters Gris, Matisse, Derain, Léger and Douanier Rousseau. He also began his important friendships with Gertrude Stein and Apollinaire.

The painting 'Les Demoiselles d'Avignon' of 1907 was possibly the single most revolutionary work of the twentieth century, and the story of its origins is now famous. Picasso began the work strongly under the influence of Cézanne's 'Bathers', and the angular,

Death of Torero, 1933, Musée Picasso, Paris

geometricized forms of the female nudes are a development of the Master of Aix's achievement, of which Picasso had been reminded at Cézanne's memorial exhibition that same year. He then left the painting for a short time, before returning a few months later to rework the two faces on the right of the canvas. There can be little doubt, despite the painter's inscrutability on this subject, that his reason for repainting the faces was his exposure to the new influence of primitive African sculpture after his visit with Apollinaire to the Musée du Trocadero.

The impact of this extraordinarily raw and powerful work is now historic. It was greeted at first with complete bewilderment, not only by critics and public, but also by fellow avant garde painters: Picasso recalls even Matisse laughing at it behind his back. Despite this initial lack of comprehension, 'Les Demoiselles' heralded the first stage of Cubism and completely revolutionized the future course of modern art. In this one startling work, Picasso had abandoned for ever the notion that it was an artist's task to record what he saw before him – and so the concept of abstract art was born. Later, in 1923, Picasso was to comment:

They speak of naturalism in opposition to modern painting. I would like to know if anyone has ever seen a natural work of art. Nature and art, being two different things, cannot be the same thing. Through art we express our conception of what nature is not.

The Cubist movement, which began with the painting of 'Les Demoiselles' in 1907, continued until the outbreak of the First World War in 1914. Its evolution was dependent both on Picasso and on the other painters who joined the group, most particularly Georges Braque, who became involved in 1908, as well as Ferdinand Léger and Juan Gris.

The origin of the movement's name has never been clear. Matisse was supposed to have remarked in front of a Braques canvas of 1908: 'Trop de cubes!', whilst other sources claim that the art critic Louis Vauxcelles wrote in his review of a Braque exhibition at Kahnweilers of 'petits cubes' and later of 'bizarreries cubes'. As so often in the history of art, it was a remark made in mockery that gave the movement its name. Cubism had three distinct phases: the Cézanne or African phase from 1907-9, the Analytical phase from 1909-12 and the Synthetic phase from 1912-14. In 1923, Picasso wrote of the movement which was to remove his name from the realms of obscurity for ever:

Maja with Doll, 1938, Musée Picasso, Paris

Many think that Cubism is an art of transition, an experiment which is to bring ulterior results. Those who think that way have not understood it. Cubism is neither a seed nor a foetus, but an art dealing primarily with forms, and when a form is realized, it is there to live its own life.

Picasso also said that he was never again to form the close friendships which he enjoyed at this time. The outbreak of war, of course, changed everybody's life. In 1916 Picasso moved out to a small suburban house in Montrouge, where he continued to work; in the following year Jean Cocteau suggested that Picasso should accompany him to Rome to make designs for the scenery and costumes for Cocteau's new ballet *Parade*, for which Erik Satie had written the music. This new association with Diaghilev's Russian Ballet brought Picasso new friends amongst musicians, artists and dancers, not least Stravinsky, Bakst and Massine. Among the troupe was a young and beautiful dancer, Olga Koklova, with whom Picasso fell in love. They married the following year and her dark, vulnerable looks became the inspiration for a series of portraits. Their son, Picasso's first child, was born in 1921.

Picasso's relationships with women are a subject in itself, and one that has attracted a good deal of attention. Apart from his two marriages (the second to Jaqueline Roque in 1961 when he was eighty), he also had long standing relationships with Marie Thérèse Walter with whom he had a daughter, Maia, born in 1935; Dora Maar with whom he lived from 1936-8; and Françoise Gilot, who bore him a son, Claude, in 1947 and a daughter, Paloma, in 1949. As an artist as well as a man, Picasso clearly needed the stimulation of new passions, and all these women, as well as others he knew, had a distinct kind of beauty which inspired a new phase in his painting.

In the years which followed, Picasso was to experiment with a wide variety of styles and media. If the definition of an artist of great genius is one who refuses to be satisfied with any one achievement but constantly pursues new directions, then Picasso might have originated it. He experimented constantly with Surrealistic, Neo-Classical, abstract and figurative concepts, as well as working as a potter and a sculptor in a variety of media.

Among Picasso's recurring motifs was the bullfight, with which he had been familiar since his childhood in Spain. The associated myths and legends were to become the background for many of his compositions. His deep-rooted feelings of patriotism for Spain also found expression in his work, reaching a climax with his famous 'Guernica' of 1936. Later, he wrote about the strong emotions which inspired this powerful work:

> In the panel on which I am working, which I shall call Guernica, and in all my recent works of art, I clearly express my abhorrence of the military caste which has sunk Spain in an ocean of pain and death.

Every phase of Picasso's working life tells a different story. He had an apparently endless flow of ideas which lasted into his nineties. It is fascinating to read what he said about his art, although it is important to remember that the artist believed strongly that, ultimately, his pictures should speak for themselves. 'They asked me why I didn't write', he said. 'It's very easy to write when you're a writer, you have the words trained and they come to your hand like birds.' But Picasso, as we know, was more than able to express his extraordinary abilities not in words, but through his art.

Self Portrait
1900

Museo Picasso, Barcelona

You're a painter, too, so you know how it goes. We can give ourselves the worst kind of trouble over our canvases, and tear our hair out, without anyone asking us to. On the contrary, nobody gives a damn whether we're doing one thing or another. And we always make the worst choice, even when we know they'd prefer a bouquet of flowers. In any case, they won't like what we do. And even if they do like it, you can be sure it won't be at all because of the painting.

I paint the way someone bites his fingernails; for me, painting is a bad habit because I don't know nor can I do anything else.

Cited in Doré-Ashton
Picasso on Art: A Selection of Views, 1972

Where do I get this power of creating and forming? I don't know. I have only one thought: work.

I paint just as I breathe. When I work, I relax; not doing anything or entertaining visitors makes me tired. It's still often 3.00am when I switch off my light.

Cited in E. Beyeler
Picasso, 1968

[19]

Harlequin, Paris Autumn
1901

The Metropolitan Museum of Art, New York
Gift of Mr and Mrs John L. Loeb, 1960

I paint only what I see. I've seen it, I've felt it, maybe differently from other epochs in my life, but I've never painted anything but what I've seen and felt. The way a painter paints is like his writing for graphologists. It's the whole man that is in it. The rest is literature, the business of commentators, of critics.

Cited in A. Jakovsky
Midis avec Picasso, 1946

Old Guitarist
1903

I don't search for anything, I try to put as much humanity as possible into my paintings. It's too bad if this offends some conventional idiolizers of the human figure. Besides, all they have to do is to look a little more attentively into a mirror ... What is a face, really? Its own photo? Its make-up? Or is it a face as painted by such or such painter? That which is in front? Inside? Behind? And the rest? Doesn't everyone look at himself in his own particular way? Deformations simply do not exist. Daumier and Lautrec saw a face differently from Ingres or Renoir, that's all. As for me, I see it this way ...

Cited in A. Jakovsky
Midis avec Picasso, 1946

La Vie, Barcelona
1903

The Cleveland Museum of Art,
Gift of the Hanna Fund

It isn't I who gave the painting that title, 'La Vie'. I certainly did not
intend to paint symbols: I simply painted images that arose in front
of my eyes; it's for the others to find a hidden meaning in them.
A painting, for me, speaks by itself; what good does it do, after all,
to impart explanations? A painter has only one language; as for
the rest ...

Cited in A. Vallentin
Picasso, 1957

Why do you think I date everything I do? Because it is not sufficient
to know an artist's works – it is also necessary to know when he did
them, why, how, under what circumstances ... Some day there will
undoubtedly be a science – it may be called the science of man –
which will seek to learn more about man in general through the
study of the creative man. I often think about such a science, and I
want to leave to posterity a documentation that will be as complete as
possible. That's why I put a date on everything I do ...

Cited in G. Brassaï
Picasso and Company, 1966

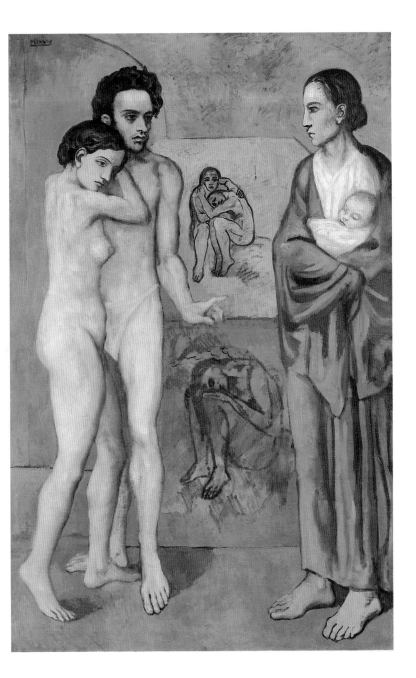

Lola, La Soeur de l'Artiste

I don't know. Ideas are just simple points of departure. It's rare for me to be able to pinpoint them, just as they came to my mind. As soon as I set to work, others seem to flow from the pen. To know what you want to draw, you have to begin drawing it. If it turns out to be a man, I draw a man – if it's a woman, I draw a woman. There's an old Spanish proverb: 'If it has a beard, it's a man; if it doesn't have a beard, it's a woman.' Or, in another version: 'If it has a beard, it's Saint Joseph; if it doesn't have a beard, it's the Virgin Mary.' Wonderful proverb, isn't it? When I have a blank sheet of paper in front of me, it runs through my head all the time. Despite any will I may have in the matter, what I express interests me more than my ideas . . .

Cited in G. Brassaï
Picasso and Company, 1966

Les Demoiselles d'Avignon

1907

'Les Demoiselles d'Avignon', how this title irritates me. Salmon invented it. You know very well that the original title from the beginning had been 'The Brothel of Avignon'. But do you know why? Because Avignon has always been a name I knew very well and is a part of my life. I lived not two steps away from the Calle d'Avignon where I used to buy my paper and my watercolours and also, as you know, the grandmother of Max came originally from Avignon. We used to make a lot of fun of this painting; one of the women in it was Max's grandmother, another one Fernande, and another one Marie Laurencin, and all of them in a brothel in Avignon.

According to my original idea, there were supposed to be men in it, by the way, you've seen the drawings. There was a student holding a skull. A seaman also. The women were eating, hence the basket of fruits which I left in the painting. Then, I changed it, and it became what it is now.

Cited in C. Zervos, 'Pablo Picasso'
Cahiers d'Art, 1935

Self Portrait

1907

National Gallery, Prague

Actually, everything depends on oneself. It's the sun in the belly with a million rays. The rest is nothing. It's only for that reason that Matisse is Matisse – it's because he carries the sun in his belly. And it's also the reason why, from time to time, something happens. The oeuvre one creates is a form of diary.

I'm no pessimist, I don't loathe art, because I couldn't live without devoting all my time to it. I love it as the only end of my life. Everything I do connected with it gives me intense pleasure.

Extract from 'Propos à Tériade'
L'Intransigeant, 15 June 1932

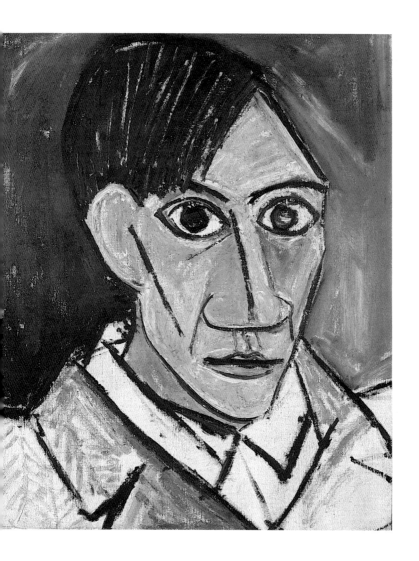

Femme à la Mandolin
1908

Christie's, London

There is no abstract art. You must always start with something. Afterward you can remove all traces of reality. There's no danger then, anyway, because the idea of the object will have left an indelible mark. It is what started the artist off, excited his ideas, and stirred up his emotions. Ideas and emotions will in the end be prisoners in his work. Whatever they do, they can't escape from the picture. They form an integral part of it, even when their presence is no longer discernible.

Cited in C. Zervos, 'Pablo Picasso'
Cahiers d'Art, 1935

Factory at the Village of Horta de Goro
1909

Hermitage, Leningrad

A picture is not thought out and settled beforehand. While it is being done it changes as one's thoughts change. And when it is finished, it still goes on changing, according to the state of mind of whoever is looking at it. A picture lives a life like a living creature, undergoing the changes imposed on us by our life from day to day. This is natural enough, as the picture lives only through the man who is looking at it.

Cited in C. Zervos, 'Pablo Picasso'
Cahiers d'Art, 1935

Study for a Construction
Pen and ink 1912

Collection, The Museum of Modern Art, New York

Look at these drawings: it's not that I intended to stylize them that they've become what they are. It's simply that the superficiality has left them. I didn't look for anything 'expressly'. . . . Evidently, there is no other key for that but poetry . . . If the lines and forms rhyme and become animated, it's like a poem. To achieve it, it is not necessary to use many words. Sometimes there is much more poetry in two or three lines than in the longest of poems.

Cited in A. Jakovsky
Midis avec Picasso, 1946

Rhythm is a perception of time. The repetition of the pattern of this wicker chair is a rhythm. The fatigue of one's hand as one draws is a perception of time.

Cited in A. Liberman, 'Picasso'
Vogue 1956

The Card Player
1913-14

Collection, The Museum of Modern Art, New York
Acquired through the Lillie P. Bliss Bequest

I who have been involved with all styles of painting can assure you that the only things that fluctuate are the waves of fashion which carry the snobs and speculators; the number of true connoisseurs remains more or less the same ...

In terms of laboratory research, the search has been thorough and intensive. Our epoch could not go any further. Certainly we have achieved a profound break with the past. The proof that the revolution has been radical is demonstrated by the fact that the words expressing fundamental concepts – drawing, composition, colour, quality – have completely changed meaning.

Cited in A. Junyent, 'A Visit with Picasso', 1934

The Violin
1914

National Museum of Modern Art, Paris

I consider a work of art as the product of calculations, calculations that are frequently unknown to the author himself. It is exactly like the carrier-pigeon, calculating his return to the loft. The calculation that precedes intelligence. Since then we have invented the compass, and radar, which enable even fools to return to their starting point. ... Or else we must suppose, as Rimbaud said, that it is the other self inside us who calculates.

Cited in Doré-Ashton
Picasso on Art: A Selection of Views, 1972

Portrait of Olga in an Armchair
1917

Musée Picasso, Paris

They speak of naturalism in opposition to modern painting. I would like to know if anyone has ever seen a natural work of art. Nature and art, being two different things, cannot be the same. Through art we express our conception of what nature is not.

Cited in Doré-Ashton
Picasso on Art: A Selection of Views, 1972

Three Musicians
1921

Philadelphia Museum of Art
A. E. Gallatin Collection

Everyone wants to understand art. Why not try to understand the songs of a bird? Why does one love the night, flowers, everything around one, without trying to understand them? But in the case of a painting people have to *understand*. If only they would realize above all that an artist works of necessity, that he himself is only a trifling bit of the world, and that no more importance should be attached to him than to plenty of other things which please us in the world, though we can't explain them. People who try to explain pictures are usually barking up the wrong tree. Gertrude Stein joyfully announced to me the other day that she had at last understood what my picture of the three musicians was meant to be. It was a still life!

Cited in C. Zervos, 'Pablo Picasso'
Cahiers d'Art, 1935

The Lovers

1923

The National Gallery of Art, Washington DC; Chester Dale Collection

In the end, there is only love. However it may be. And they ought to put out the eyes of painters as they do goldfinches in order that they can sing better.

Extract from 'Propose à Tériade'
L'Intransigeant, 15 June 1932

Madame Picasso
1923

National Gallery of Art, Washington DC; Chester Dale Collection

That's the marvellous thing with Frenhofer in the *Chef d'Oeuvre Inconnu* by Balzac. At the end, nobody can see anything except himself. Thanks to the never-ending search for reality, he ends in black obscurity. There are so many realities that in trying to encompass them all one ends in darkness. That is why, when one paints a portrait, one must stop somewhere, in a sort of caricature. Otherwise there would be nothing left at the end.

Cited in D. Kahnweiler
Interviews with Picasso, 1959

[49]

Paolo as a Harlequin
1924

Musée Picasso, Paris

Contrary to what sometimes happens in music, miracle children do not exist in painting. What might be taken for a precocious genius is *the genius of childhood*. When the child grows up, it disappears without a trace. It may happen that this boy will become a real painter some day, or even a great painter. But then he will have to begin everything again, from zero. As for me, I didn't have this genius. My first drawings could never be exhibited in an exposition of children's drawings. The awkwardness and naïveté of childhood were almost absent from them. I outgrew the period of that marvellous vision very rapidly. At that boy's age I was making drawings that were completely academic. Their precision, their exactitude, frightens me. My father was a professor of drawing, and it was probably he who pushed me prematurely in that direction.

Cited in G. Brassaï
Picasso and Company, 1966

Three Dancers
1925

Tate Gallery, London

I'm always saying to myself: 'That's not right yet. You can do better.' It's rare when I can prevent myself from taking a thing up again ... x number of times, the same thing. Sometimes, it becomes an absolute obsession. But for that matter, why would anyone work, if not for that? To express the same thing, but express it better. It's always necessary to seek for perfection. Obviously, for us, this word no longer has the same meaning. To me, it means: from one canvas to the next, always go further, further ...

Cited in G. Brassaï
Picasso and Company, 1966

Seated Bather

1930

Collection, The Museum of Modern Art, New York
Mrs Simon Guggenheim Fund

I want to say the nude. I don't want to do a nude as a nude. I want only to *say* breast, *say* foot, *say* hand or belly. To find the way to say it – that's enough. I don't want to *paint* the nude from head to foot, but succeed in *saying*. That's what I want. When one is talking about it, a single word is enough. For you, one look and the nude tells you what she is, without verbiage.

Cited in C. Zervos, 'Pablo Picasso'
Cahiers d'Art, 1935

Paysage Boisgeloup

You have to turn in order to paint the landscape with your eyes. To see a thing you have to see all of it. Landscapes must be painted with the eyes and not with the prejudices that are in our heads. Perhaps not with the eyes closed, but with the eyes ... [pointing to a porcelain form on the high-tension wires in the foreground]. It would be nice to paint only detail. But in order to understand it and transform it into an image, it is necessary to paint the entire vista which makes it exist like this. It is not possible to paint it directly without all its infinite relationships. Once I painted an interminable landscape: hills, terraces, sea, trees and I don't know what all. At a certain point I found on my way a fish. I painted it with great attention, avidly. At the end I realized that all the rest wasn't the least bit important to me. I wanted to paint precisely that fish. But the fish alone I would not have known how to see.

Cited in Doré-Ashton
Picasso on Art: A Selection of Views, 1972

La Muse
1935

National Museum of Modern Art, Paris

I have a horror of people who speak about the beautiful. What is the beautiful? One must speak of problems in painting!

Paintings are but research and experiment.

I never do a painting as a work of art. All of them are researches. I search incessantly and there is a logical sequence in all this research. That is why I number them. It's an experiment in time. I number them and date them. Maybe one day someone will be grateful.

Cited in A. Liberman, 'Picasso'
Vogue, 1956

La Guernica
1937

Museo Nacional del Prado, Madrid

No, the bull is not fascism, but it is brutality and darkness.

My work is not symbolic. Only the Guernica mural is symbolic. But in the case of the mural, that is allegoric. That's the reason I've

used the horse, the bull and so on. The mural is for the definite expression and solution of a problem and that is why I used symbolism.

Cited in C. Zervos, 'Pablo Picasso'
Cahiers d'Art, 1935

Dora Maar
1938

Tate Gallery, London

When you start with a portrait and search for a pure form, a clear volume, through successive eliminations, you arrive inevitably at the egg. Likewise, starting with the egg and following the same process in reverse, one finishes with the portrait. But art, I believe, escapes these simplistic exercises which consist in going from one extreme to the other. It's necessary to know when to stop.

Extract from 'Propos à Tériade'
L'Intransigeant, 15 June 1932

Woman in a Fish Hat

1942

Stedelijk Museum, Amsterdam

Beauty is something strange, don't you find? To me it is a word without sense because I do not know where its meaning comes from or where it leads to. Do you know exactly where its opposite is to be found? If someone were to show me that there exists a positive ugliness, that would be something else. Of course, I know very well what they would tell me; for after all, these words are bogey men to frighten the children of the art schools and the rest. The Academy devised the formula; not long ago they submitted the senses to the 'official' judgement of what is beautiful and what is ugly. The Renaissance invented the size of noses. Since then reality has gone to the devil.

Cited in J. Sabartés
Picasso, Portraits et Souvenirs, 1946

La Casserole Emaillée
1945

National Museum of Modern Art, Paris

I see for others, that is to say, in order to put on canvas the sudden apparitions which come to me, I don't know in advance what I am going to put on canvas any more than I decide beforehand what colours I am going to use. While I am working I am not conscious of what I am putting on the canvas. Each time I undertake to paint a picture I have a sensation of leaping into space. I never know whether I shall fall on my feet. It is only later that I begin to estimate more exactly the effect of my work.

Cited in C. Zervos, 'Pablo Picasso'
Cahiers d'Art, 1935

Goat's Skull, Bottle and Candle
1952

Tate Gallery, London

Some people call my work for a period 'surrealism.' I am not a surrealist. I have never been out of reality. I have always been in the essence of reality [literally the 'real of reality']. If someone wished to express war it might be more elegant and literary to make a bow and arrow because that is more aesthetic, but for me, if I want to express war, I'll use a machine-gun! Now is the time in this period of changes and revolution to use a revolutionary manner of painting and not to paint like before.

Cited in C. Zervos, 'Pablo Picasso'
Cahiers d'Art, 1935

Bearded Man

A few strokes of a brush that have no meaning will never make a picture. I do this sort of thing myself, and occasionally you might say it was an abstract. But my brushstrokes always signify something: a bull, an arena, the sea, the mountains, the crowd... To arrive at abstraction, it is always necessary to begin with a concrete reality... Art is a language of symbols. When I pronounce the word 'man', I call up a picture of man; the word has become the symbol of man. It does not represent him as photography could. Two holes – that's the symbol for the face, enough to evoke it without representing it... But isn't it strange that it can be done through such simple means? Two holes; that's abstract enough if you consider the complexity of man... Whatever is most abstract may perhaps be the summit of reality..."

Cited in G. Brassaï
Picasso and Company, 1966

[71]

Jacqueline in a Mantilla

Private Collection

It's not important to me to know whether a certain portrait is a good likeness or not. Years, centuries pass, and it is not important if the physiognomical traits are exactly those of the person portrayed. The artist loses himself in a futile effort if he wants to be realistic. The work can be beautiful even if it doesn't have a conventional likeness.

Cited in F. Del Pomar
Con las Barscadores del Camino, 1932

[73]

The Artist and his Model
c1963

Art is never chaste, we forbid it to the ignorant innocents, never allow a contact with it to those not sufficiently prepared. Yes, art is dangerous. And, if it's chaste it isn't art.

Cited in A. Vallentin
Picasso, 1957

Self Portrait
1972

Courtesy, Fuji Television Gallery, Tokyo

It's not what the artist *does* that counts, but what he *is*. Cézanne would never have interested me a bit if he had lived and thought like Jacques Émile Blanche, even if the apple he painted had been ten times as beautiful. What forces our interest is Cézanne's anxiety – that's Cézanne's lesson; the torments of Van Gogh – that is the actual drama of the man. The rest is a sham.

Cited in C. Zervos, 'Pablo Picasso'
Cahiers d'Art, 1935

And those men lived in unbelievable solitude which was perhaps a blessing to them, even if it was their misfortune too. Is there anything more dangerous than sympathetic understanding? Especially as it doesn't exist. It's almost always wrong. You think you aren't alone. And really you're more alone than you were before.

Cited in H. Parmelin
Picasso Dit, 1966

[77]

CHRONOLOGY

Pablo Picasso
1881-1973

1881   Born in Malaga.

1895-1904   Spends time in Barcelona, where he first makes contact with avant garde ideas.

1901-4   Settles in Paris. Blue Period.

1904   Settles in Montmartre, where he lives on and off until 1945. Mixes with a circle of writers: Apollinaire, Rousseau, Derain and Gertrude Stein.

1904-6   Rose Period.

1906   Meets Matisse and Gris.

1907   Meets Braque.

1909-14   Cubist Period.

1917   Visits Italy, working with Cocteau and Diaghilev on the ballet *Parade*.

1918   Marries Olga Koklova. Son born in 1921.

1919   Meets Miro.

1920-5	Neo-Classical paintings.
1925	In contact with Surrealists.
1932	Buys château at Beisgeloup. Begins sculpting plastic heads and iron sculptures.
1933	Begins etchings of The Sculptures Studio.
1935	Daughter Maia born to Marie Thérèse Walter, his model.
1936-8	Lives with Dora Maar, his model for many paintings and drawings.
1936	Appointed Director of the Prado Museum at the outbreak of the Spanish Civil War.
1937	Exhibits 'Guernica' at the Paris World Fair. Never returns to Spain after this. Visits Paul Klee in Switzerland.
1939-45	Remains working in Paris during the German Occupation.
1946-8	Lives in Antibes with Françoise Gilot.
1947	Son Claude born.
1949	Daughter Paloma born.
1948-51	Takes active part in Peace Congresses throughout Europe. Clouzot's film *Le Mystère de Picasso* released.
1953	Separates from Françoise Gilot.
1955	Moves to Cannes.
1958	Buys Château de Vauvenargues near Aix.
1961	Marries Jaqueline Roque.
1973	Dies in the South of France aged ninety-two.

ACKNOWLEDGEMENTS

The editor and publishers would like to thank the following for their help in providing the photographs of paintings reproduced in this book:

Art Institute of Chicago (p23)
Bridgeman Art Library (pp27, 33, 35, 41, 43, 45, 57, 71, 73, 75)
Fuji Television Gallery, Tokyo (p77)
Metropolitan Museum of Art, New York (p21)
Museo Nacional del Prado, Madrid (pp62/63)
Museo Picasso, Barcelona (p19)
Museum of Modern Art, New York (cover, pp9, 29, 37, 39, 41, 57)

National Gallery of Art, Washington DC (pp49, 51)
National Gallery, London (p7)
National Gallery, Prague (p31)
National Museum of Modern Art, Paris (pp61, 69)
Philadelphia Museum of Art (p47)
Photo RMN (frontispiece, pp13, 15, 53)
Stedelijk Museum, Amsterdam (p67)
Tate Gallery, London (pp8, 55, 65, 71)
The Cleveland Museum of Art (p25)

We would also like to thank the publishers of the following books for access to the material contained in them which has been reproduced in this volume:

Con las Barscadores del Camino F. Del Pomar, Ediciones Ulises, Madrid 1932
Interviews with Picasso D. Kahnweiler, Jahresring, Stuttgart 1959
Midis avec Picasso A. Jakovsky, Arts de France, Paris 1946
'Pablo Picasso' C. Zervos in *Cahiers d'Art* 1935
Picasso E. Beyeler, Basel Editions, 1968
'Picasso' A. Liberman in *Vogue*, New York 1956
Picasso A. Vallentin, Albin Michel, Paris 1957
Picasso and Company G. Brassai, Doubleday, New York 1966
Picasso Dit H. Parmelin, Gothier, Paris 1966
Picasso, Portraits et Souvenirs J. Sabartés, Louis Carré et Maximilien Vox, Paris 1946
Picasso on Art: A Selection of Views Doré-Ashton, Viking Press 1972
'Propos à Teriade' in *L'Intransigeant,* 15 June 1932
A Visit with Picasso A. Junyent, Mirador, Barcelona 1934

Every effort has been made to contact the owners of the copyright of all the information contained in this book, but if, for any reason, any acknowledgements have been omitted, the publishers ask those concerned to contact them.